POETIC VIEW

MUNIM KHAN

Printed in the Islamic Republic of Pakistan.

Printed: July, 2022
Edition: 1st
ISBN: 978-969-749-191-9
Price: Rs 1200 PKR, $12 US

www.auraqpublications.com | raabta@auraqpublications.com
@AuraqPublications | @AuraqBooks | +92-300-0571-530
Printed and Bound by ***Passive Printers*** - www.passiveprinters.com

Poetic View

This droplet of my journey as a poet and writer is the courage and inducement from the dazzling ladies in my life:

Saima Ali khan the marvelous mother RIP

Ms Afifa Anjum

Dr Zakia Anjum

Ms Shakeela Anjum

Ms Sadia Anjum

The great aunts that one can wish for.

CONTENTS

PART 1

"ANIMATIVE VIEW"

LOST YOU

Tears fell off;

My cheeks all red

Not quite me for oft

I was pushed and i was led;

Towards your corpse's feet that felt frost

You were laid on a bed

Touched your hands that felt soft

You lied! that you won't die

You went off without a bye

I was scared

My feet bared my weight

All eyes on me, for which i didn't cared

For i maybe the next bait

Than i remembered to compensate

You told me that, for you knew your fate

But still you lied! That you won't die

You went off without a bye

I watched you for some time

Some voices called my name

They carried me away

Your grave was ready in-time

You were settled down and laid;

On andesite and tiles

I wished you stayed

Even though I wasn't at the funeral, far some miles

"You lied! That you won't die

You went off without a bye"

AN OLD FRIEND!

-Walking past a territory

-A wealthy bit off home

-Build with care was it two story

-Lived in it a person, who was alone

-Not currently in sight, but enlightened was his glory

-But before him, all was simple

-All before him, lived in it was my pal with a cheek dimple

-We would play catch within the fences

-He'd cheat but i was cool with it

-Having sword fights and defenses

-With only sticks and no such kit

-I'd beat him yet always, was he calm and charmed

-As before, all was simple

-There lived my pal with a cheek dimple

-Remembering all the gatherings, funerals, memorials

-We would slide through the back door

-Just to watch our preferred serials

-We were introverts, better off than to explore

-We had ourselves, we had each other

-As before, all was simple

-As lived in that home was my pal with a cheek dimple

-I asked that man

-Rather i could revisit our childhood

-He approved of my plan

-Now i entered our little hood

-And dreamt of you being there

-You were there all along, but it was not simple

-You were my only pal with a cheek dimple

LAD ON A CAMEL

A startled face

Worn, still forward looking

Ears sharp, just in case

Eyes haunting

Fierce mind

Lies bind, to this man

Looking forward to what he can

Or what he is capable of

In a fury, self-theory

There he goes (cried the vagrant)

He jaunts as though he is the Sargent

Vigorous as a sprite

A spirit to fight

Careworn as though a sin be omened

up against his will; summoned

In a fury, self-theory

Behold the prodigious insight

Along himself he ferried

A bloke to bet on

A comeliness of its kind

Something quite breezy to find

In a fury, self-theory

A tale and a bend

My encounter with consciousness
Not urging for my anima
Being indebted yet heartless
Appealing yet dissonant dilemma
Myself to wander and surpass
Isn't one me in strain
My head in vertigo
Fall of grieve to and fro
Dull yet finer than viciousness

A point to ponder
Swarm of grace and colder
To whimper such louder
Making others frowner
Being myself, prouder
I ain't though the founder
Just the astonisher

BE OVER FLAWS!

Appears though you're scared
You're broken and in pain
You haven't been properly cared
Whatever you do, its all vain
You haven't talked and shared;
As though your opinions are chained
Guessed that you've been compared;
From whom you failed

Quite frankly, you waited;
But became more opinionated

Some doubted your perception
Others walled your motive
They offered you correction
But no one was promotive
What you needed was acception

Enough of being notive

Put an end to all misconceptions

And start being assertive

Quite frankly, you wasted

All your devotions towards being opinionated

Hopeless

Can't figure out what I'm viewing

Dusk or dawn?

I'm sitting while my mind is brewing

I'll think until I yawn

Than I'll curl up to a corner

And be just a mourner

"I'm hopeless mi amour"

Hopeless

Can't figure out how to converse my thoughts;

Into something colorful and odourful

But I have flaws

I'm dreadful without any laws

I'll take a sip from the mug of cry;

It's all I can afford and buy

"I'm hopeless mi amour"

Hopeless

Some hope

Surrounded by options
Imposing answers
Called by many captions
Pointing at my manners
They were perfect;
I was barely adequate

Then came my soul with goals
It said they were a lie
That I was the loftiest
They were the slightest
I was told as I had ambitions
"I ***Had hope***"

Was i any positive
Or was that all an adrenaline
For sure I was hiding and fugitive
Though I was a moraline;
Because I had ambitions
"***I Had hope***"

I Live there

Gusts and gale
Wheat-grass all pale
Ready for reaping
Yet no sign of ranching

The tower mill I see
Over by the hill far from sea
The huts on mountains, down and by the gully's glee
Icecaps runny along the steep rubble and andesite
All as clear as some sight

Though feels solitary
Empty and desolate
Creeps my dear soul;
This was once a place of chores
Not comfortably airy
Can't explain the stat
It's all lown

*_ But was once my lawn_*

I'm dimming

Am I delusional

Is there a way to cruise away in life

Probably a way that's suitable

That provides a route to a prize

Though I feel frail;

I feel ill

Am I diseased

But ain't that rare till my mid life

Though I'm illusional

Is this my after life

Cz I feel frail

I feel ill

Am I (that soon) relieved

Cause I'm not yet revived more thrived

Is it due to my confusion, elusion or conclusions

Or am I the only one alive

Is it over yet

Seeing that I feel frail

I feel ill

Late Night walk

Moon being itself
On a cold damp night
Seeing stars glow
With perfection yet bright light
My voice stuttering
To this fascination
The clouds as though they disappeared

I wondered and grudged
Sighed and indulged
Towards the may and might
Along with my compeer
Letting my doubts ignite
It was what i could bare
And talk violently with share
Along with the complementation of the sight

A pleasure to be yourself

With someone who's considerate

No hour rush, no minute buzz, no time late

Just a few individuals,

Admiring life with a perspective of a gods one

LIFE

Time, time is relevant

Passes by like a dragonfly

But never comes saying it's good bye

Yet we feel responsible for the past

But you can do nothing about it at last

And yet we do sins;

That have no such fins

And carry out the duables and proximations

That are to be written by god

At last it is human who faces consequences

And behold the authority of god

And yet we do sins;

That have no such fins

Sorrow is what others say

What I say is it is the corrections, mistakes to be done
 and much more to be learned

In the end it is god who we are to answer

Life is a joke for people with blindness

And not blindness as in blind

It is the sins in sorrow

So why we commit sins

That have no such fins

THE NAMELESS BOY

-Was there someone like this boy
-Who thought it every single day
-The day of salvation for him
-Was the day of irritation for him
-Lost misguided, struggler; toddler was this boy
-but was still his mum's boy

-Little he knew about life and death
-But one thing was sure;
-His heart was cure
-The struggles he for-taken
-The life for he was given
-By the one, the giver

-A life cost for him
-A lost mum for him
-Was he the one chosen;
-Or the one
-Ever did he do such sin
-Cost his life a lost kin

His Mums Salvation

-His life begins

-His thoughts dissolve

-His eyes devours

-His mind be folds

-The life he thought;

-Was nothing but a file of salvation

-Morning to morning

-Fear gaining his heart

-Reminding a day to make his mum proud

-He knew, the boy knew the consequences his life will forgive

-He knew the boy knew that life will be cruel to him

-But never told anyone as the fear gaining his heart had a sudden escape

-Thoughts escaped the boy

-And now was he in peace and in joy

-And finally the day came; When his mum was gone

-His thoughts changed

-His mind diffused

-Madness filled the boys heart

-But one thing the boy knew;

-That his mum was proud

-A hill to mount

-A life to count

-Dreams to be haunted

-Things to be sorted

-But the boy knew;

-His mum was proud

-Doubts he had

-Thoughts that mislead him

-The boy knew, that life was a surprise

-And he was to surpass

-Life goes on; so don't let those thoughts get you

-Because when you let fear;

-Then there is no room for light

-The tears the boy lead

-The mind he fed

-With thoughts that were mean

-He knew that life was mean but the path -was clean

-And the boy foretold himself to continue the path

-And the boy finally came to know;

-That his mum was proud

Nameless boy V 2.0

Dispassing the life
Mentality so shy
Elevation so high
Motivation as low
Beginning to cry;
Is the nameless boy

Judgement so neigh
Mind so crumb
Nothing to do but sigh
Settling himself to be dumb
And beginning to cry;
Is the nameless boy

Confusing thoughts
Circulation shots
Sadness inhaled
Deepness exhaled

Focus away

Towards a way

To make his day

Suddenly stuck in a wave

That faroshes the may

And all he does is cry

And he is the one;

The nameless boy

Nameless boy V.03

The dreams I saw
The hardship I took
The earness I looked
The mindset I grew;
Were never ever the part of my life before

The judgements they made
The criticism I accepted
The challenges I completed
The obstacles I passed;
Were never ever the part of my life before

And at last I stand be hearted
Still stubborn to some,
Though nice to ones;
That embraced me from inside out
They think I was cut out

Lesser they knew about the emotions I held

The more they knew, the more it hurt

Was i the first to see a chance in life

Or the last to see my mum fade apart

Still all of this: “was never ever a part of my life before”

Nameless boy v.04

Distant in a valley
The pictures and the days
Far into moonlight
A lonely home was a place;
Diamonds may them be ahead;
Heading out of town;
Enough of this dread

Sorcering his way,
Darting in some sights
Hope-wishing by the orbs;
Flashing light into bay
Zis farming his own mind
His own crafts used along
Imagining himself out of dawn;
Dusk was perfect to be gone!

Nameless boy v.5

Fear, was it over?

I, in a fleat ,did I do the wrong?

Did I happen to be more sober?

Is it stretched out all long?

Frightening wisdom follow me..

Will it conjure, will it hollow me?

Thoughts, did it change?

Was it all a mystery?

Dots thy exchanged;

Is it visible, they be a victory?

Satan follow me..

Will you dare to swallow me?

Fame, did I shine?;

My own self in a corner

Is there any fine?;

For my job of being a mourner

Nameless boy !, follow me..

Will you pray ?;

Will you be down on your knees?

Promises to keep…many of them

Damp all the trees

Bitter all the glees

Zephyr settling up

Ice making my foots to a stop

Internally it's wicked;

By my point on running barefoot

Externally i'm all uproot

Stood up and in a look

For my promises far ahead

Promises far ahead

Its eerie I'll say again

Barely with a "***can***"

I feel my huffs

All my pauses and the puffs

Feeling the gore in my veins

Along my brain that explains;

That it might start to have strokes and migraines

But i continue with all the pains

since i have promises far ahead

Promises far ahead

Its near i can see

The place of promises

Yet nowhere are my promises

Are they nothing but debri

They felt solid all before

In hundreds and galore

Yet now I'm lost

With no fortune nor any cost

Still i will follow for my promises far ahead

Promises far ahead

Sunrise typical

Intruding into them dorms
Hunting for my intellect
Rushing into the getup
The pound being a teacup;
Served by those floweret
Wholly rinsed in the bathe
Motionless on the tutorage
Gnashing on them flower baked biscuits
Provisional as though being elequent

Laces unlaced
Darting for the van
Floating through street lane
Entered the camper with haste
Sat on the lead
Rasping his hand and feet
Bone chilling sun-up;
Yet everyone off to chores

Hushed yet overloaded day

Not neglecting the sea bay

Just a stripler going to tutelage

Creak Of buses' exhaust

Doorway ungaping

In comes the frost,

Straightaway face taping.

Gate of the alma mater opening

Watch man out of his shack

Greeting and waiting on those icy plams

Children pushing there way with charm

It's a Day to be educated;

Enlightened and formed

A stripling bunch , going to tutelage

False accuses

I fell in a ditch today

I need to back myself

I fell in a ravine of thoughts today

I need to rescue myself

I was accused today; of being all fragile today

I need to carry myself

I fell to a garden of plays today

I need to checkmate myself

But there's no point in embracing myself

Instead I must insist myself

To walk the path of honour;

As of today,all of it was no meaningful thing to me

New year

It's the end of the year;
still no sign of flakes

The silenced streets
And no one as dear
There's dimming of light
On Christmas tree bright
There's colors all around
And No amusing sound

It's the end of the year;
Still no sign of flakes

Firecrackers crackling them tones
Rallying people on bridges and highways
Expecting the charms and pleasures

They got frauded

Just a new year

No sign of brand new

It's the end of the year

Still no sign of flakes

What we caused

In the hallow night

Led by the darkness

Was once seeked upon light

That perished with mankind's stubbornness

The floods were the meanfulness

Adversity were the beauty

But anger was click to end

The surroundings questioning the morrow

Atmosphere filled with sorrow

One thing that spread;

Was gladness, hatred and sadness,

Other is cruelty

Hurting ain't an art, nor a beauty

Though love is a heartless feeling;

Which will summarize your life into one hell of a journey.

“But make sure to keep your heart cure and secure from those who might hurt it”

Thinking at times

-Tick of time, or the drop of tap

-They sound familiar

-Won't let anyone to a nap

-Making us somewhat peculiar

-In the nightfall, with lights switched out;

-Leaving us with thoughts to sort out

-both may stop soon,

-They may stop soon

-Sip of beer, or chip of lead

-They leave an echo

-Remembering of all the dread

-Making us forget what we know

-While sitting at a bar;

-Murmuring of those afar

-Both may stop soon

-They may stop soon

-Water dripping;

From a cold wet cloth

-Smells dreadful, the gauze, after sniffing

-Eventually the odor fades;

-Leaving my hand, (to the cloth),clinging

-A stream of liquid passing through my hand,

-Rather it's the blood or the water from the cloth

-Though Both may stop soon,

-They may stop soon

Not trustworthy

-There flew by

-Where I lay

-Were they joying in sunshine

-Though I sat with sigh

-And I stood by the bay

-While they got themselves, with colours, dyed

-Though I could only get myself to lie

-It looked pleasing

-Somewhat teasing

-On my deep, dark soul of deeds

-As I see life like beads

-In pieces, I see such beauty

-Yet who're worthy to the fullest;

-Can't see the half of what I feel, mean and lead

-Still at that time;

-I could only get myself to lie

Lotus land

I dreamt of being on a lotus land

More like a far land

With the surface of a hard sand

It was unmanned

But all of it was alluring

It had a lake with a water flow

And ravines so low

Quite the trees, ever so green

Though my mind being not as mean

As it wasn't to be found

It was just me and my heart

And my admirations to this astonishing place

It was truly admirable

A rainbow quite colorful

Hidden behind a steep mountain of rock full

It was all mindful

But was also divine

Aurora being fascinating

Eyes weren't but sogging

It was a dare to blink

As the sight was to be sighed

To just lay on the greenery

And engross the scenery

With such raised ego

And much less time;

Until you're devoured by dirt

Let your mind set free

So it seems freshness in beauty;

And witnesses the enchantment just like the heart

It isn't a crime for your wit to be in awe

It will only make it educate

Won't make your heart saturate

But will further be spirited;

"And for all be liberated"

A look from the window

I see the light shining bright

It may shine more of might

Weaker it gets, more it's sadder

You see stars apart from each other

It looks like they just had a fight

Just admire the view;

Through the window of sight

(Crickets singing)

(Birds dozing)

Clouds colliding and banging

Leaves twisting and swirling to the wind

Ears filled with so called "*life sounding*"

It's sometimes frowning

But most of the time, sighing

Just admire the view;

Through the window of sight

There's the residence of the squirrels

Abandoned and nestless

As they found some new place to call "***home***";

And to sleep into each other's cozed up furs,

Wheezing and purrs

It's all awing

Most of the time, heartwarming

Though it's all sightseeing

Just admire the view;

Through the window of sight

Annihilation on call

They adopted miseries oncoming miseries
They were stump like feathers and lashes
Roaming badges, willy blooded coffins
Whimpers and cries
Good byes from their gens
Yet to save them was caution
Behind hand to capture foes now
It was already a bloodshed
Pool of whimpering flesh
Bothered thoughts in me
Was it all calculated

"Or was the genocide, a holocaust type coincidence"

Be some example flourish

There's something about the tip of this pen

It's perishing

Like a heart unnourishing

It's out of spot

Just as the dreams that I crop

It's out of images

Roughly to be vintage

It's collapsing; unthriving

There's something about the taste of my zen

There's this outright strength

Which makes me rational

Yet supposedly passional

Not currently, any how

It's leaving my anima; I'm done reviving

Heritage and endless

There are errors

Then there are tempers

We see recent through mirrors

They explain the changeovers;

That we wear per diems

starting the day with an outlook;

That we catch from a Brooke

That Brooke has memories

It's full of documentaries;

That defies one's being

That defies one's being

All amend the known globe does

It's what it wants to perform

It's why they have the badges;

All lust and thirst

All dust and untrust

Can't be undone

Can't be unseen

Unfortunately;

It defies one's being

It defies one's being

POV ON MY SOUL,A HARSH ONE

Shadows explain
My Demon's claim over me
It occurs mostly often
But why blossom
Why lonesome
Carried some, heart some
Why much sublime
My heart can't go like that
Somehow it has
Somehow it can
Somehow it will
Surely it must

An appeal I give;
To my soul with sores
Must I have an evening store
Where my bare heart mourns
Why painfully

Why stain full

Yet deserving

My heart can't beat like that

Though it has

Somehow it can

And it will

Surely it must

TIME

By my wrist, there's a watch
It shows the moon's and midnights
It left on my wrist, a scratch
Though I wear it to find moonlight;
Or even sunlight!
My shoulders are on a dark side
While time is my only bride

There are cultures in my town
That explain importance of time
Though I sit on my lawn
And try to write any rhyme
I just had a breakdown
Cz my shoulders are on dark side
While time is my only bride

I AS A STONE

Holding onto the stone

Gripping onto it's cracks

Was it hit or sawn

It's hard as a bone;

And broke as a lone

I am the stone

And I'm not a worthy known

I'm lost within the marbles

Will someone notice?

That I'm not within their Brahman

I might just have to protest;

So that I'm listed as a re-examine

I am the stone

And I'm not a worthy known

I'm tickled and delighted

Even if I'm not

I'm newly sighted

And I'm a cute mascot

I'm cramped yet mightier

Cz I am the stone

And I'm not a worthy known

A SINNER

I requested her presence

From the author and the creator

All I wanted was her essence

But the supreme(God,)was my hater

All I witnessed was her absence

But I was told; I was no greater

I was a sinner

And she was no listener

I was on a life –sentence

Declared by a dictator

They said they found an evidence;

That proved I was a traitor

All I knew were the consequence

And now I was no longer; someone's complainer

I was a sinner

While she was all a winner

SHORE

-I'm by the sea shore
-Thoughty on my life goal
-Nevertheless my heart felt a sore
-Felt as though; disappeared my soul
-Now I was a carcass with hollow core
-But you don't know; what I have in store

-I'm by the gully's wideness
-Thoughty about my life's role
-When I was suddenly hit by blindness
-Now I cannot watch and adore
-I just want to go home
-And I'll be my own console

-I'm by the monument;
-That eroded in a fight
-I can't find any document
-That says it's right; the genocide
-I don't have an extra magic door
-That'll lead me back to along shore

WEATHER'S EFFECT

It's raining its stormy
The lightning and all cloudy
All frightening cz I'm lonely
Less brightening causing anxiety
Its all bland
Nowhere near what i planned

I'm aiming at my enemy
Assuming its mandatory
He's begging to live amaturely
But im lacking confidence to kill him, not manly
Maybe I'm insane
And he's all humane

I'm canning someone named lonely
He's caring but not homely
He says he's sailing through tough times, recently
He hasn't been laughing lately
Says weather's not pleasant
Makes me wanna take an antidepressant

NOTIVE – NOT NOTICED

Catching upon the memories
Upon a mountain with echoes
Hearing within sounds of breeze
There by seeing, circling crows
I began being notive
In somewhat of cognitive

Some harsh, mostly brutal;
My ideas they are
Yet for me they are crucial
Pardon for those if it's lethal
I've just begun being notive
In somewhat of cognitive

That a vessel or a capsule?
On a mission or not really?
Figuring it out like a fool

Looks like a star, though barely

Am I going lunatic?

Or have I just become being notive

In somewhat of cognitive

JUST SOME POLLUTANTS

There's been an outbreak;
A viral microscopic virus
Demoliting it looks like a piece of cake
Until we all are in aww and in silence
For that it is inevitible, for Gods sake!
The next thing we hear are sirens
That warn us to be educated and awake
It is no pandemic
Maybe a disorder or just a headache

I feel a warm coarse in my veins
I feel hot but need a blanket for the cold
I lay down and enjoy a bottle of Champaign;
Along that i nab on a bread having mold
Its old yet that's only what i can afford
Not including the Champaign in my budget
Everyone can buy that, even a midget
I pray and say Ameen
For the meal and the famine!

NO LAWS DO I HAVE!

I was left off in an ocean
The tides washing off my sins
Saving myself was my devotion
Wrinkles appearing on my skin
Whales, carrying out their locomotion
Though i have no fins
Neither any wings
So can't escape my flaws
I can't escape my flaws

I was carried away by blossom
Promising me that my diseases will be cured
I touched the flowers with caution
But they turned into mortals, and i knew I was lured!
Though it was only my notive,for future precautions
I was confirmed and assured
That I don't have a stem
So i can't grow any flaws
I can't grow any flaws

I DEMAND

I ask you this inquiry
About which you may have some queries
Would you ever want to die?
In this unwelcome environment
Would you ever want to lie
About your assignment
That you burned without getting concerned
But either way you learned;
You can move without hesitation
“you're eager to change;
You're eager to have a rage”

Again, I ask you a question
For which you may have a suggestion
Should I cry
In this rasping domain
Or, rather greet a bye
And head out in a train
But either way I will turn;

My lonely new home into a barn
As I have moved without hesitation
"As I'm eager to change;
I'm eager to have a rage"

hope: A downfall and a slope

Subjected to hope
There being no reply
Being misguided in a loop
Though not nearby
So, do i cope?
Or slide down a great slope

Belief, believing it
Yet no accord
Quit, quitting it
As for all, no horde
Living in a dictionary;
Of no man's boat
So, do i cope?
Or slide down a great slope

Failed miserably…

I got lost on the pride
The state of mind in paradise
Being polished and sacrificed
Non is my part in any advice
I tried but failed miserably
I have failed miserably

A cost to be paid
Be a man is what they said
I was all the time, in fade
Non is my word in being afraid
I tried but failed miserably
I have failed miserably

Affirmative over the lead
Being an outcast with no deed
I was suffering, I was in need
I wanted to be saved, to be freed

I tried but failed miserably

I have failed miserably

A growth of mind

Where ever i thought, i couldn't find;

Any of the beauties of the kind

As i had ended up a blind.

I tried but failed miserably

I have failed miserably

In pain by the cuffs

The emotions being as tough

Non of it being enough

There was me with my packed up stuff

I tried but failed miserably

I have failed miserably

The world has been a crime of freaks!

Maybe I'm losing this contest;

For the piece of luck and bread

I've been willing to be blessed;

Just to be fed

Never felt the one neither the best

Lost hope on myself, on my self-story

Counting years till i lose my modesty

I carry out this discussion

Why ive been kept in no justice

Maybe just a precaution

Or to win the fixture

My life feels the distortion

Lost hope on myself, on my self-story

Counting years till i lose my modesty

I have found myself a being

She then calls me a lost one

I have to be in between my fleeing

Yet its too late, I haven't even begun

Wish i could be unseeing;

I could be the person knowing none

Lost hope on myself, on my self-story

Counting years till i lose my modesty

A martyred soul

Dragged on within the rails

I'm blocked up and in chains

Try to rescue myself;

Yet fails

Try to crawl but have too much sprains

Felt the bruises and fractured bones

I can't but live off the loans

Hanged down a steep hill

The screams and pain

Barely in sight, a windmill

There by seeing the sins, once again

I was wanted to be dead and killed

But couldn't wash out my crimes;

As they were already drained

I could feel the bruises and fractured bones

I cant but live off the loans

In scarcity of alrighty

Refreshment of breaths

Asserting a mind thought

Feeling calm in hospitality;

yet in strength

Reminding the brutality;

yet in fear of being caught

A cold nighty,

And I am trying to be the righty

Solid witnesses i may have provided;

Not enough for my phycology

As i was wrongly guided

With pride and under the astrology

Resulting in all what my eyes did

Gazing upon the truth of ecology

A cold nighty,

And I am trying to be the righty

Watching all the happenings
Waiting by the hilly sides and;
killing all the time i have left
Passing by the castle's gates
In memory of my state it was
The trees be piling up on dates and;
Sweetness of it making some cause;
Making a difference
I walk pass the town of greatness;
Maybe its adored
Hailing of the mightiness, of my lord

The greenery of the bushes and shrubs and;
The calling of the birds to a feast
I wander in an awe to be astonished, admonished
Though it won't make things better, not a least
All the wishes be in a corner, all of may be cared
As I'm walking past the town of greatness;
Maybe its adored
Hailing of the mightiness, of my lord

PART 2

"CHARMING VIEW"

Enjoy the EVE

I'll go with you
Even though it's thinkable
I can summon monstrosity for you
Though it's unfavorable
I have plans for us
However I won't be accessible
A delectable eve is it
Except I'm not looking forward to it
I'll rather hover in my place at present

Ain't much I can conclude
As I'm having no mood
Though I have tasks to achieve
Then go I; for a dive
It's a shame I'm muddling
In spite of that you're stunning
Go and adore the eve;
While I hover in my place at present

Maybe we are doves....

Adores the dove
From a hundred miles away
Fluttering high above
Within the cold gust of bay
Might it just be in cuffs
Might it just be in love

Herons singing history;
Depends on the melody
Squirrels up the nest and;
The turtles nap on sand
Might it just be a bit of snuff
Might it just be a bit of love

Maybe they want the error
Maybe they are a fault
Maybe it's a mystery;
Maybe love's a victory
It's a never ending meal
Maybe love's a fantasy

I'm different

I'm isolated

Was i sophisticated

Or sarcastic

Neither ironic

More alarming, calming, charming

Though am i

May I conclude

My settlement to you

“I'm in my youth

My fears are sub due

My roots aren't you

They're sovereign and glued

I have no ego

Neither some amigo

Just a regular boy”

Though am i

Sighing my life

-Me writing a glimpse;

-Of my life so slim

-And think so thick

- Even then so calm

-Dreaming a shore

-With a kin by side

-No ignorance and gratitude

-Just us and you;

-Fixing life's meaning with you

So think of a way

That we can attain

To reach our thoughts;

Is a mount full of stops

Don't worry, a way will provide itself

That will ruin the ones

Trying to teach us the wrong

And far away we go;

Into twilight.

Where no ignorance and gratitude

Only us and you;

Fixing life's meaning with you

Begins love at a sight (first sight)

Crucial love, first sight

Feels overwhelming

Brutal gain of certainty(trust)

Feels blundering(awkward)

Humane empathy(feeling)

Feels gratifying(satisfaction)

Sentimental changes

It's all in one sight, all in one

Beginner's love it is;

love for most

Keen juveniles(teens)

Their adorations towards their adorable

It's full of atmospheric beauty

Gladdening sight

Brightened hearts

It's in one sight, all in one

Beginner's love it is;

love for most

I wish for first conversation

I'll scribble words coming from you
I desire and please a convenient
Excuse for our conversation
Though I will love to see you in red and blue
Seeing you look a sensation
Is it true what you do
Prying on me...
Well it's my craft and not yours

You just look good in magnanimity
While I'm all lousy analytically
I'll wait years for you statistically
But will ya remember me,in curiosity

I'm officially a bummer
A runner not a stunner
Though you don't go for looks
You go for links; of attraction and love

HURT AND PAIN

I went passed you
Your feet touching my shoe
You shook a might
Which made a sign for me to sight
yet,we both were on different lane
Providing me with nothing but pain

Gosh! I peaked
You thought of me as a freak
I begged and begged;
For rather I was correct
You knew I was a seeker
Maybe your Future keeper
But you said no:
As we both were on different lane
Providing me with nothing but pain

BY YOUR SIDE!

I worship, a stone wall

Behind a huge mall

Where we had those brawls

We were not friends over all;

But we met when we could only crawl

You were the one who would call

When you were down and in a fall

You would cry on problems such small

And surely i know it all

But why now do i recall

Them sensitive features of yours

Agreeing to the terms;

Won't make things better

Running wont erode them

Facing it won't decode them

Dealing with it, burns

Though from it will we learn;

To be stern and blunt

I'll have my goals, alongside no adore

But for you, my core

Be near, so i can recall

Them sensitive features of yours

I could've asked!

I wouldn't ask her out
That'll be humiliation
It won't take long, no doubt
But wont i experience suffocation
Waiting for the inner voice to shout
Depending on the situation
Won't open, the jaws of my mouth
Won't let me talk
So i couldn't ask her out for a walk

You would wave
Tell me its a bye
Advising me to behave
But I'll think of it as a lie
You said I'm no brave
But i will try to deny
You told me i stalk
But I'll say just let me talk
So i could ask you out for a walk

STILL WITH YOU,FOR YOU!

The days went by

When we had a good time

Laying on the grass, sighing the sky

Caring no more about sunshine

We would wait for the night;

And then adventure into the might

I was there before

I'm still with you

Still for you

You know I'll be in my lawn

Staring at the sky till dawn

Now we look away

Mostly you do that

I wait for you to look back

But then you forget

Now we wait for the morning

So we can ignore the night

Our bond may not be concerning

But i know, it gives you a fright

As you know i was there before

And I'm still with you

Still for you

If you need me I'll be in my lawn

Looking at the sky till dawn

For you i walk miles!

This town, is wide enough

Been searching around for you

I know that I'm no tough

But I'll walk till i find you

You and your soul too!

I beg your pardon

Are you calling me a burden?

I'll move out from your house

You're no longer my spouse

Ill live within the streets

Colder nights and bare feet

The quite roads, no one as dear

Then may i come back to you in fear?

I will even walk till i find you

You and your lost soul too!

You'll open the door

Call me a freak and shout:

"How many times have i told you before;

I don't need you anymore"

I try to remind you of our past

And that you didn't asked

Yet i wanted to tell you;

That i have walked a long way to find you

You and your soul too!

To you, i write

I know it'll bother you

But may i ask

I kinda have a shadow following you around

It has a mask

Rest is me and I've drowned

Drowned in the gorgeousness

That has become my addictiveness

You brought colors

To that shadow

Even it asked

Can i buy her those flowers

Purple and magenta

It'll be a way to have her in my hands

As it's the only thing i can fix and made it my agenda

You made me drown in the gorgeousness

That has become my addictiveness

Leave with him

Those hands have a gesture

They look light and pale

May i take them in my hands

They'll be free and would sail

I would hold them up till i fail

I can't hold them up for long

They belong to someone else

They are for someone else

Those eyes have a color

Reminding me of your lover

He wants your presence;

But you are talking to me

He wants your acceptance;

Are you ready to agree

Cause your hands belong to someone else

They are for someone else

He warned me today

That i shouldn't be in your way

He cursed me out

Screamed to his open mouth

I told him you are his

It's the truth, its what it is

I know you belong to someone else

You are for someone else

Living for you!

You went off to a god

Leaving nothing but despair

Now I am called a fraud

This isn't to me; any fair

I want both of us to be applaud

By the gusts and dead air

I just wanted to make you proud

But couldn't find a way that'll be loud

I write within my voice

I might choke on the lies

But I have no other choice;

But to pick paths with no such joys

I just want both of us to be applaud

By the gusts and dead air

I just wanted to make you proud

But couldn't find a way that'll be loud

herself!

Lost by the waters of grace
The elegance of herself
Its finesse its no craze;
As I can see my book on your shelf
I'm lost within the phrase:
"There's no more in our case"

I'm lost within the tides and waves
The truth within herself
Its growth of her wounds;
And not any of her craves
All might be one day; in bounds
Which will make me lose my cave
It had all the memories in a safe

I'm lost within the lilies
The delight within herself
It's her words not the breeze
She is alone, a oneself

And i come to a stop and lost;

That she is done for with her blood

I am lost within the horns;

A not so delectable eve for herself

It is she in a dress in torns

While he can't be in a zone, himself

I end up in a mind so lost;

That they both may lose their trust; In the frost

Herself v.2

Poet be but harmless

Inconsistent towards his works

Poet be but charmless

His thought hurts

A poet be but armless

On his hands written the verse

A poet wanting her;

To take the pill of curse

The sounds be echoless

His mind be gloomy

The waves be tideless

His heart be droopy

Legs be tireless

Continuing to walk a beauty

A poet wants her;

To take the pill of curse

"He finds hope in her mansion
A few drops of compassion
A poet can't feel or have any anticipation;
Towards the sorrow, in her wound of laceration"

Herself v.3

Wheels go by…
She waited by
Lurking her ears;
Steaming her to cry
Barren was the land
Empty her hand
I walked by;
Saving her not to die…

Stumbled she…
Helped her to her feet
Shouts and the pants
Screaming and the vain
Cornering herself
Lowering her gaze
Tormenting herself
Hiding her craze
She wanted herself;
Spending night with own self

LIMERENCIA

Aligns all the stars

Beneath that my manners

Losing the art on guitar

The name spotted on the banners;

Have i been seeing, the name of yours

Have I been in state of limerence lately?

Even if i was;

It did no good, sadly

Surrounded, in somewhat of war;

Representing the memories

A remembrance or a glance

Not known when'll be the next chance

Have i been seeing, the image of yours

Have I been in state of limerence lately?

Even if i was;

It did no good, sadly

Busied in some chores

Fuzzy beneath the skull

Dancing by the wind

Sobbing to be a find

Have i been seeing, the dull charm of yours

Have i been in state of limerence lately?

Even if i was;

It did no good, sadly

Cursed attachment

Her gaze, his eyes

Reflecting twinkle all around

His hands, her hands,

Palm to palm;

Spatting their secrets all around

Taking laughing and most of all adore it all

Their differences were their similarities

Her beauty,his thoughts

In the evening glow;

of horizon light

Suffered were they

By those who discouraged, disgusted, disgraced them by their ways;

About their feelings

More than feelings but griefings

They knew it was possible

Yet others said impossible

And here were they

Talking about it all

In the evening glow;

Of horizon light

God made them one

Happy were they, of what the do

After all it was darly,

It was honey,

It was sweet.

Her gaze lowering his

Her smile, his day begins

Her tears, his sadness

And they were one, for sure

No more a secret, their truth

Their decision was healing of their bruise

No doubt they excluded those who were far from talking to

They were finally one, they were

Her gaze twinkling his;

In the evening glow of horizon light

Be back by dark!

Left the stove on

Be back in a time

Left dishes on table-top

Be back by light!

Leave the lights on

It's better to know you're there;

I'll be back by dark!

Thy love i saw

Bitter was it not

Never i saw any flaw;

Pure you were, adverse not

You left a spot in the moonlight!

Marking lines through dots

You waited for me to come back;

But i was stuck in moon's delight

Don't wait for me' sleep well

I'll be back by dark!

"Words Straight from the heart touch the soul of the reader and that's what you did. You have dig out an incredible talent of yours for which she and all of us feel proud. This marvelous journey with your soul will teach you tremendous lessons to grow as a human".

(Afifa Anjum Khattak IMS UOP)

"My mind is wide open so I should think clearly
For I don't know when it is going to last
Munim Khan

"A mother's presence is a blessing that all we need, but her love and prayers will always surround and protect you. You followed her vision beautifully and wrote incredible words for her. I feel pride and appreciate your effort with prayers that it opens other doors of success and prosperity in future, Amin"

(Dr Zahid Ali Khan MS WAPDA Hospital Mangla)

"Munim is an amateur poet who has used his emotions in words that connects his spirit with the reader making us feel what he never showed in a very unique and elegant way. Dear you must continue on this path for youll do very well"

(Shakeela Anjum Khattak Pharmacist & Manager UNPeace Keeping)

Printed and Bound by ***Passive Printers*** - www.passiveprinters.com
Printing press that offers Print on Demand (POD) Facility.
Printed in The Islamic Republic of Pakistan.

www.ingramcontent.com/pod-product-compliance
Lightning Source LLC
LaVergne TN
LVHW041115150826
845673LV00007B/2057

* 9 7 8 9 6 9 7 4 9 1 9 1 9 *